KENGO KUMA

IN TOKYO

with over 40 illustrations

KENGO KUMA

MY LIFE AS AN ARCHITECT IN TOKYO

CONTENTS

INTRODUCTION

I was born in an area between Tokyo and Yokohama that did not belong to either city. Ever since I was a small child, I would ride the Toyoko line, which connects these two great metropolises, when I was out and about, as an integral part of my daily life.

I became a 'border person', as defined by the sociologist and philosopher Max Weber, viewing Tokyo from an outsider's perspective. Observing the city while walking around its streets enabled me to discover a wide variety of locations, cultures and people, and that Tokyo is a collection of small villages, rather than one big city.

When designing the National Stadium (p. 42) for the 2020 Tokyo Olympics, rescheduled for 2021, I focused on creating something that would be in keeping with the surrounding neighbourhoods of Aoyama, Sendagaya and Gaien, rather than something that was representative of Japan as a whole. We achieved this by drilling down into the essence of these different 'villages'. When I design a building, in any city, I believe that the world is a collection of villages, instead of a group of nations.

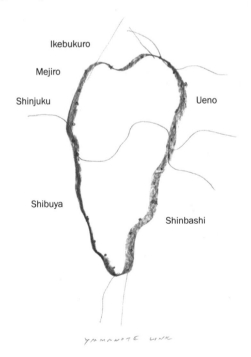

Ikebukuro

Mejiro

Shinjuku

Ueno

Shibuya

Shinbashi

YAMANOTE LINE

YOYOGI NATIONAL GYMNASIUM

Built as the swimming and diving venue
for the 1964 Tokyo Olympics, the Yoyogi
National Gymnasium, designed by Kenzō
Tange (1913–2005), became a symbol
of the event. By hosting the Olympic
Games, Japan was showing the world it
had fully recovered from the destruction
it had sustained during the war.

Other projects completed in
time for the Games include the Tōkaidō
Shinkansen, the world's fastest railway
at the time, and the Shuto Expressway,
a network of motorways built in the
sky above Tokyo, which featured in the
Soviet sci-fi film *Solaris* (1972). Another
building, the Komazawa Gymnasium,
a stunning concrete tower designed
by Yoshinobu Ashihara (1918–2003), was
inspired by pagoda design and hosted
the wrestling events.

The year 1964 also marked
the peak of Japan's rapid economic
development, the result of a deliberate
process of industrialization undertaken
with unusual speed. This exultant
national mood was translated splendidly
into architectural form by Tange, who
led the modernist movement in postwar

Japan. Known as 'the world's Tange', he designed buildings in over thirty countries, and was seen as having an uncanny ability to accurately predict and interpret the spirit of the age.

Anticipating that the height of buildings would increase across Japan, Tange proposed a vertically orientated design for the Yoyogi National Gymnasium, with two concrete towers and a roof suspended between them. Japanese cities at the time were made up entirely of wooden structures, one or two storeys high, and this striking design stood out dramatically. (Japan's first skyscraper, the Kasumigaseki Building, wasn't completed until four years later, in 1968.)

The gymnasium's structure was supported by a system used primarily in civil-engineering projects like suspension bridges. Tange's daring design earned widespread praise, and seemed to be showing the world that Japanese technology had caught up with that of the West. The beautiful sweeping curve of the roof has been compared to the gentle curves of the Golden Hall (*kondō*) of Tōshōdai-ji, the famous eighth-century temple at Nara, while the supporting pillars appear to be influenced by the *chigi* (forked roof finials) of buildings such as the Ise Grand Shrine in Mie Prefecture. Tange's great talent lay in combining traditional Japanese aesthetics with cutting-edge architectural techniques.

Our design for the National Stadium (p. 42), the centrepiece for the second Tokyo Olympics in 2021, was also very inspired by traditional Japanese architecture. But while Tange aspired to verticality, we looked to horizontality, believing that pre-1964 Tokyo, with its low wooden silhouettes, was a better model for the city of the future.

Even after the 1964 Olympics were over, I was unable to get Tange's gymnasium out of my mind, and at weekends I would travel by train from Yokohama to swim in the building. Watching the light falling from the top of the beautiful arched ceiling made me feel as if I was in heaven. As I swam silently, I would think to myself how I, too, wanted to create buildings that would, someday, move people in this way.

The 1964 Tokyo Olympics marked the peak of Japan's economic development ... This exultant national mood was translated splendidly into architectural form by Kenzō Tange.

SHIBUYA

In his book *Empire of Signs* (1970), the French philosopher Roland Barthes wrote that the centre of Tokyo is occupied by a void. Unlike European cities, where the central area is marked by an architectural focal point, such as a castle or a church, it is a quiet forest that lies at Tokyo's heart – home to the Imperial Palace, residence of the Emperor, surrounded by over 1 km^2 (0.4 sq miles) of parkland and gardens.

Barthes saw this as underlining how the structure of society and the urban landscape differ greatly between Japan and the West. The centre of Tokyo is certainly a void, but one that is protected by a circular train line, the Yamanote (see p. 7), which forms a 40-km (25-mile) loop around it. It seems to me that this ring of steel emphasizes the importance of the void, and the depth of its significance.

An empty void in a city's central space is far more welcoming than any towering building. The Yamanote line passes through a number of terminal stations – Shibuya, Shinjuku (p. 56), Ikebukuro (p. 64) – connecting up with the private railway lines that run out to the suburbs. It is used by over two million passengers each day. Around the empty centre formed by the palace grounds, these stations serve as the hubs of Tokyo's financial and cultural activity.

Shibuya, in particular, is the centre of youth culture, and where I would go, from my childhood onwards, to hang out. On Hallowe'en, great numbers of youngsters in costumes gather round the station, drinking and singing until morning. Hallowe'en in Shibuya, in fact, could be called Japan's biggest festival.

I was in charge of designing the new station for Shibuya. Above it is Shibuya Scramble Square (see p. 15), a tower stretching 230 m (over 750 ft) in the air, its base formed from interlocking curved planes, which give a scooped-out appearance. Wanting to create a tower that spilled over with a sense of speed and noise befitting the area, we printed the glass with ceramic powder to create stripes, as if the energy of the neighbourhood's street culture extended into the sky. On the top floor is an observatory designed by Nikken Sekkei, with views across the city.

At Shibuya station, get on the Tōyoko line. After about ten minutes, you will arrive at Den-en-chōfu, a neighbourhood known for its radial pattern of streets, rare in Japan, and where I attended nursery and primary school. The industrialist Eiichi Shibusawa, seen by many as symbolic of the Meiji era (1868–1912) and the father of capitalism in Japan, was so impressed by the writings of Ebenezer Howard, the founder of the UK's garden-city movement in the nineteenth century, that in the early 1900s he developed Den-en-chōfu as a garden suburb of Tokyo. I was also much influenced by Howard's ideas, which I had learned about at school.

The playground where I used to play with my friends as a child is on the neighbourhood's south side, beside the Tama River. This has now become Seseragi Park; at one of its corners stands a library that I designed, constructed from wood. It blends seamlessly with the park around it, so that visitors can enjoy the sensation of reading a book while being in the middle of a forest.

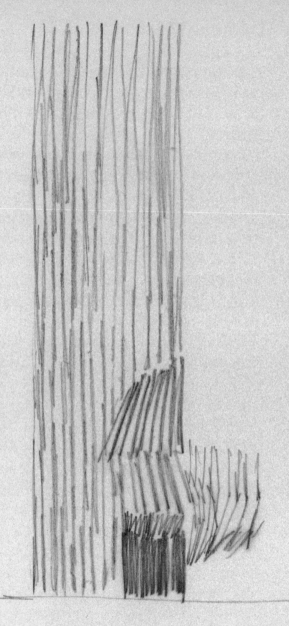

SHIBUYA SCRAMBLE SQUARE

DAIKAN-YAMA

The commercial district of Daikan-yama
is an upscale residential area in Shibuya
(p. 12). It was the appearance of Hillside
Terrace, a multi-purpose complex
designed by Fumihiko Maki (b. 1928) and
built over a thirty-year period, between
1969 and 1998, which ensured this
formerly quiet enclave became the city's
most desirable neighbourhood.

Maki, along with Arata Isozaki
(b. 1931) and Kishō Kurokawa (1934–
2007), was a student of Kenzō Tange,
and clearly inherited the master's
fascination with urban design. But he
was critical of the ubiquitous Tange-
style design of the 1960s, which he
termed 'megastructure' architecture,
and proposed instead a gentler, more
intimate way of designing residential
complexes, or 'group form', of which
Hillside Terrace is a prime example.
(Incidentally, the first article that I ever
wrote was about Hillside Terrace.)

Tange designed cities that
revolved around a defined axis, along
which he would position buildings of
a symbolic and monumental nature
– appropriate, he believed, for Japan

during its period of accelerated economic growth. The rebuilding of Hiroshima following the devastation of the atomic bomb is the best example of megastructure architecture and Tange's philosophy of urban planning.

Maki searched for a design typology that was more human in scale, and suited to the calmer, more mature Japan that emerged after the years of growth came to an end. After Hillside Terrace, located beside a main road, with buildings not exceeding 10 m (33 ft) in height, was built, Daikan-yama was transformed into a stylish and popular neighbourhood. With its traditional small wooden houses converted into shops and restaurants, it became the hip place for young people to go.

Heading downhill in a southerly direction, you arrive at the Meguro River, where, in the past, a number of small factories were clustered together along its banks. This part of Tokyo comprises two different zones: Daikan-yama, which still retains the upscale feel of the residential district, and Nakameguro, on the other side of the river, which has much more of a working-class feel. In recent decades, in cities across the world, industrial zones beside rivers and canals have become the focus of attention, with their unique vivacity associated with places where things are made. Several other industrial neighbourhoods remain in Tokyo, including Ōta, beside the Haneda Aiport; and Oshiage, which spreads out beneath the Tokyo Skytree (2011), designed by Tadao Andō (b. 1941).

A little further up the river is the Starbucks Reserve Roastery (2019), which we designed. In the atrium is a huge coffee roaster, 10 m (33 ft) in height. Because the area is designated as a semi-industrial zone, we were able to get away with such an enormous machine inside the building. In Oshiage, we designed the hotel One@Tokyo (2017), with a rooftop terrace from which visitors can enjoy views of the city's factories, and the Tokyo Skytree at night.

Fumihiko Maki proposed a gentler, more intimate way of designing residential complexes, or 'group form', of which Hillside Terrace is a prime example.

ONE OMOTESANDŌ

Prior to 1964, Omotesandō was a quiet *sandō*, or sacred path leading up to a shrine, lined with Japanese elm trees and devoid of shops and restaurants. Dating from 1919, it leads to Tokyo's biggest shrine, Meiji Jingū (p. 24). On the far side of the shrine is Tange's Yoyogi National Gymnasium (p. 8), where Omotesandō begins to shift from sacred path to the city's foremost fashion street. At the very top of the street is One Omotesandō, our headquarters for the LVMH group, a world leader in the fashion industry, which was completed in 2003.

Omotesandō itself is lined with the flagship stores of fashion brands from around the world. Christian Dior (2004), designed by SANAA, has an otherworldly transparency created through a combination of glass and acrylic panels, while Prada, designed by Herzog & de Meuron, is cloaked by a curtain wall of diamond-shaped panes of curved glass (Jacques Herzog noted that his aim was to create a sensual form that would appeal to women). Miu Miu, also designed by Herzog & de Meuron, features a façade with an emphasis on slanting lines, recalling the roofs of Japan's shrines and temples. One street back is the Neil Barrett boutique, designed by Zaha Hadid, where organically shaped walls made from Corian assert their presence beyond the glass.

With its row of Japanese elms, Omotesandō has a mystical feeling about it. Even today, it serves as the main approach to the shrine, so I wanted to create something with a wooden façade, like a *hokora*, or miniature shrine, in the middle of the woods. Unlike the religious buildings of the Christian or Islamic faiths, Japanese shrines are not built to honour a single deity, but many. The main shrine honours the principal god associated with it, while the *hokora* is usually dedicated to minor spirits. The architecture is secondary to the woods, and the buildings must be discreet and human in scale, so as not to intrude upon the atmosphere of the forest. I have learned much from Japanese shrine architecture.

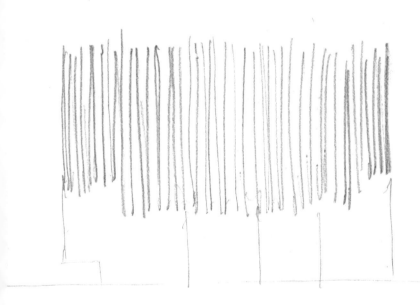

ONE OMOTESANDŌ

隈
研
吾
東
京

Our design for One Omotesandō is covered in wooden louvres made from larch, with each piece of wood forming a wedge-like shape, keeping the tips as thin as possible. These thin lines echo the delicacy of the bark of the Japanese elm trees in front of the building. The upper part of the structure cantilevers out, so that the glass-fronted meeting room appears to float in mid-air. We created this glass box as another *hokora* – connected to, but separate from, the main building.

Wooden louvres on the façade of the building echo the bark of the Japanese elm trees outside (opposite).

隈
研
吾
東
京

MEIJI JINGU MUSEUM

MEIJI JINGŪ MUSEUM

Meiji Jingū, built in 1920 and dedicated to the deified spirits of the Emperor Meiji (1852–1912) and Empress Shōken (1849–1914), is the most important shrine in Tokyo. Each January, over three million visitors come to pray for good fortune for the coming year, a custom known as *hatsu-mōde* ('first shrine visit'). They throw a coin into a box in front of the shrine, clap their hands in prayer and buy a *hamaya* (an arrow to exorcise evil spirits), before returning home.

When I was a child, there were two rituals associated with New Year's: *hatsu-mōde* and *dezomeshiki*, which has a long history that dates back to the Edo period, when Tokyo was built almost entirely from wood. Fires would frequently break out, and fire-fighters, wearing *happi* coats, enjoyed a kind of celebrity status. During the *dezomeshiki*, modern fire-fighters give acrobatic performances at the top of ladders. I always preferred going to see the *dezomeshiki*.

The grounds of the shrine may look like a primitive forest, but it was previously just a grassy plain, with hardly any trees at all. The landscape architect Seiroku Honda (1866–1952), who had studied forestry in Germany, was tasked with creating a forest that would be appropriate to the building. At the time, it was common to plant cedar trees around shrines, but Honda chose to plant a number of different species, mostly broad-leaved ones, and planted a landscape that, in less than a hundred years, evolved into a mature forest in the middle of the city. Trees were contributed from across Japan, and planted by volunteers who also came from around the country.

Today the woodland, as well as being a sacred place and home to an assortment of wildlife, is known as the forest that never dies. During the Second World War, Shintō shrines were targeted during air raids, and over a thousand firebombs were dropped on Meiji Jingū. The architect Antonin Raymond, who lived and worked in Japan during the 1920s and '30s, returned to America during the war, where his architectural

Low eaves help the building dissolve into the forest
(above). The gaps between the flanges in the ceiling are
filled with cypress to soften the space (overleaf).

practice produced a number of prefabricated homes for the US Army. He was asked to build a series of typical Japanese houses in the Utah desert, on which a new type of incendiary weapon could be tested. Yet even these specially designed firebombs couldn't destroy the woodlands surrounding the Meiji shrine.

In the centre of the forest is the *sandō*, leading up to the shrine. It follows an L-shaped curve, and is very different to the straight processional pathways found in religious buildings in the West or in China. Curves ensure that the view changes constantly, helping visitors make the transition to a deeper, more spiritual place. In the middle of the *sandō* is the *shinkyō* ('sacred bridge'), and tucked discreetly beside it is the building that we designed: the Meiji Jingū Museum. We felt that, here, the sacred forest had to play the main role, and that the building needed to recede into it.

The roofs of Japanese buildings can be divided into three types: *kirizuma* (gable); *yosemune* (hipped); and *irimoya* (hip-and-gable). The first two are often seen in Europe and China, but the *irimoya* roof is unique to Japan. Like the hipped roof, the eaves are low, allowing the building to blend into its surroundings, while creating height at the centre. (The tea houses at the Katsura Imperial Villa have roofs of this kind.) The museum's outer walls are made from specially treated dark grey metal, constructed to create a slightly textural feel (*yamato-hari*). 'Yamato' derives from the former name for Nara, Japan's ancient capital; it is a technique that is frequently found in old shrines and streets. Inside, the slender columns supporting the museum generate a sense of rhythm. They are made from a combination of steel and wood, like Tange's gymnasium (see p. 8) nearby. Inside, the desk, pencils and other items used by the Meiji Emperor are on display.

NEZU MUSEUM

This museum of ancient Japanese and Asian art and traditional handicrafts is located near the eastern end of Omotesandō, Tokyo's best-known shopping street. It was established in 1941 as the Nezu Institute of Fine Arts by businessman, politician and philanthropist Kaichirō Nezu, who founded the Tōbu Railway, in the grounds of the family home. The current director, Kōichi Nezu, is his grandson.

In 2006 the museum was closed for renovation, and we were asked to design a completely new building. To begin with, we focused on the path leading up to the museum. In the design of Japanese tea houses, the building is seen as less important than the path (*roji*) leading up to it, and tea masters of the past believed that the journey along the *roji* allowed participants to better immerse themselves in the slow time of the tea ceremony. We designed a long walkway, with visitors covering a distance of 50 m (164 ft), before entering the building beneath the deep eaves, which protrude 4 m (13 ft) from the façade. We wanted them to savour the shadows cast by the eaves, and to enjoy the bamboo wall to the left and grove to the right, leaving the noise from the crowded high street behind and quieting their minds before stepping inside.

In renovating the large tiled roof, we abstracted the detail at the top and along the edges to give a contemporary feel, while staying within the bounds of tradition. I felt that the extended eaves, which created deep shadows, were the most important feature of the building. One of the most important literary figures in Japan of the twentieth century, Juni'chirō Tanizaki, wrote an essay, *In Praise of Shadows* (1933), in which he maintained that the beauty of traditional architecture derives from its use of shadow. It proved to be hugely influential in the architectural world, as well as the literary one. Le Corbusier, the greatest architect of the last century, noted that 'architecture is the learned game, correct and magnificent, of forms assembled in the light', demonstrating to what extent

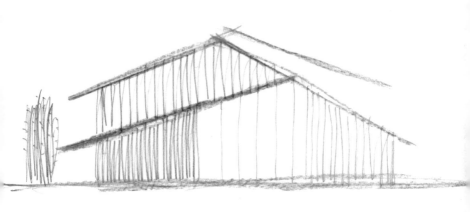

NEZU MUSEUM

light had been prioritized in the Western tradition. Tanizaki, on the other hand, spoke of the importance of shadows, of extended eaves. Rather than the light that shines directly into a room, he praised the soft light that penetrates a space after being reflected off the floor, and again from the ceiling.

In the museum's garden are four tea houses and the Nezu Café pavilion. Tea ceremonies are held frequently, and, unusually, one of the tea houses has been built as a boat floating on the lake. The lake is seen as a very important part of Japanese gardens; at the tearoom at Katsura Imperial Villa, for example, the nobility would sail boats on the river as they sipped their tea. The café was erected in the place where the Nezu family house stood, and the stove they used is still there, unchanged, giving visitors an insight into the lives of the former residents.

The unique roof design (above), assisted by large glass openings (overleaf), help to merge the outside with the building itself and the artwork inside.

SUNNY HILLS

SUNNY HILLS

This shop selling Taiwanese pineapple cake is located in the backstreets of Aoyama, a wealthy neighbourhood in the Minato district of Tokyo. Throughout the city, you just have to step away from the main road to find yourself in a maze of narrow alleyways and small houses, which date from the Edo period. The buildings that line these little streets are still mostly made from wood, and the contrast between the main roads and these alleys is one of things that makes the city so distinctive.

Sunny Hills faces onto one of these narrow alleyways, so we decided to be brave, design something on a small scale, and build it entirely from natural materials. Having heard that the shop used only the best-quality pineapple, the finest Échiré butter and sel de Guérande for their cakes, I came up with the idea of using the finest natural materials for the building as well. I wanted to weave fine strips of Japanese cypress together to create a forest-like space in the middle of the city, allowing patrons to feel as if the sun was filtering through the trees. We used delicate strips of wood, with a cross-section of 6 × 6 cm (2¼ × 2¼ in.), joining them using a traditional technique known as *jigoku-gumi* (or 'hell's interlock'), thus creating a three-storey building without the need for large columns.

Once assembled, the wood cannot be dismantled. The technique is so difficult to master that it is usually only used in furniture and fittings – I believe this might be the first time it has been used for an entire building. We used a similar construction technique in 2011 for the Starbucks in front of the Dazaifu Tenman-gū shrine in Fukuoka. Eight years later, I would design the Starbucks Reserve Roastery in Nakameguro (see p. 18) on the banks of the Meguro River. The first Roastery was in Seattle, with ours the fifth to date (following Shanghai, New York and Milan). Here, visitors can drink Japanese tea, have light meals and drink alcohol until late at night. The shop also sells beautiful products made from natural materials, created by superb Japanese artisans specially chosen by us.

In the nineteenth and twentieth centuries, the areas around rivers and canals, once the main channels of distribution, became industrial zones. Being noisy and smoky, these places were not seen as suitable for habitation or commerce, and were often overlooked. Even now, there is the distinct feel of the urban factory about them. But today, these waterside districts are enjoying a comeback, and are in the process of being transformed into fashionable, stylish places in which to work and live.

In Tokyo, this is happening in the neighbourhood around the Kanda River, from Edogawabashi to Kandabashi, and along the Meguro River. Cherry trees line the banks of the Meguro, and during cherry-blossom season, their petals are scattered across the water's surface, creating a dream-like sight. On top of the hill, to the north of the river, is the exclusive hilltop neighbourhood of Daikan-yama (p. 16), full of classy boutiques and condominiums, with Hillside Terrace, designed by Fumihiko Maki, at its heart. Indeed, Daikan-yama and Nakameguro, on the other side of the river, provide perfect examples of Tokyo's most exclusive and least upmarket neighbourhoods, respectively.

This system of wood construction (opposite) is more often used for furniture. Using it for the whole building allowed us to create a warm, friendly space (overleaf).

NATIONAL STADIUM

This new stadium, which will serve as the main venue for the Tokyo Olympics in 2021, sits in the middle of the forest surrounding Meiji Jingū (see p. 24). The inner part of the woodland, the *naien*, is where the main building of the shrine stands. The stadium sits on the east side of the *naien*, where there are a number of other sports facilities, including the Yoyogi National Gymnasium (p. 8), designed by Kenzō Tange and built for the Tokyo Olympics in 1964.

When designing the new stadium, along with Taisei Corporation and Asuka Sekkei, our priority was to ensure that it blended in with the landscape. First, we decided to keep the height as low as possible. The lighting towers for the previous stadium were 60 m (nearly 200 ft) in height, and Zaha Hadid's initial design, which was aborted after construction costs exceeded the budget, were 75 m (over 245 ft). By placing seating as close to the ground as possible, and keeping the height of the supporting truss to a minimum, we were able to keep the total height under 50 m (164 ft). During the twentieth century, much importance was attached to things that were big and tall, but, as we moved into the twenty-first century, I felt that being big and tall had become embarrassing.

We thought about what kind of year 2020 would be, and what building material would be suitable. Tange, Japan's twentieth-century 'starchitect', had designed his gymnasium during the peak of the country's economic growth; the Tōkaidō Shinkansen and the network of concrete motorways flying through the Tokyo skyline were also built then. It was a festival that celebrated industrialization, and would show the world that Japan had fully recovered from the war. But these Olympics will take place at a time when the country has an aging society, a dwindling birthrate and a shrinking economy. The event needs to be softer and gentler, symbolizing slow growth and environmental sustainability. The only material that seemed appropriate to use was wood.

Through a cycle of planting trees, harvesting them for building materials, and planting again, Japan was able to maintain its wood resources. In the twentieth century, however, concrete and steel played a major role in construction, and even when using timber, people turned to cheap sources from overseas. Japan's forests consequently fell into ruin. Trees extract carbon dioxide from the air, but this capacity is impaired in forests that have been abandoned. Woodlands that have been allowed to run wild lose their water-retention capabilities, one of the factors in the frequent recurrence of flooding, and are also linked to pollen allergies, particularly cedar.

To return the country's woodlands to a healthy condition, we need to use their wood in construction by building smaller, human-scale structures, and to manage that use carefully. The stadium's external wall uses cedar from all forty-seven of Japan's prefectures, and the roof is supported by a hybrid structure of wood and steel. Encircling the building are five-storey wooden eaves, with the wood beneath the eaves protected from sun and rain, so that it lasts longer (the seventh-century Hōryū-ji Temple, the world's oldest known wooden building, is protected by similar eaves). The eaves have cedar boards 10.5 cm (4 in.) wide, the same width used for columns and rafters in traditional wooden homes, and which the Japanese people have the greatest familiarity with.

In old buildings, small cracks were left between these pieces of wood to allow air into the room, with the width of the cracks varying according to the position of the wood. These tiny ventilation shafts help people endure the summer heat even without air-conditioning. An 850 m (2,790 ft)-long pedestrian concourse, the Sky Forest, hovers 30 m (nearly 100 ft) above the ground. Even on days when the stadium is not being used for sports events, locals can look out onto the beautiful forest of the Meiji Jingū below. The National Stadium has been built not only for sporting events, but also for the everyday lives of local residents.

NATIONAL

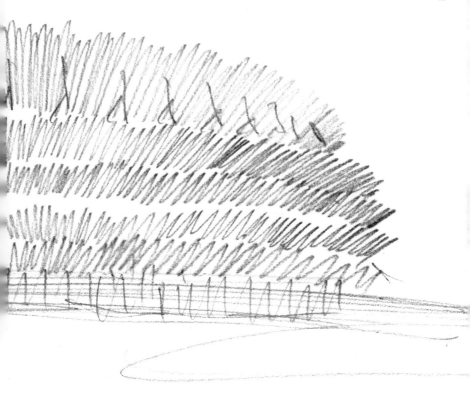

S. TADIUM

SUNTORY MUSEUM OF ART

When I was young, the Roppongi neighbourhood was home to
the *Stars and Stripes* newspaper building, and had a building
with a heliport for the US troops. In the evening, the area would
be filled with young foreigners, walking around and drinking
in the *izakayas* until morning, and as a student, I would go
bar-hopping there, soaking up the atmosphere. There is still
a slightly seedy feeling to the neighbourhoods around the
numerous American military bases in Japan, which is different
to the nightlife districts frequented by locals. Tokyo Midtown –
a mixed-use development that includes the Suntory Museum of
Art – was once the site of the Ministry of Defense, and some of
that military-base feel still lingers.

I spent six years of my youth attending Eiko Gakuen,
a Jesuit school in Kamakura. Yokosuka, another US military
base, is nearby. You can still experience that same atmosphere
in places like Okinawa, Iwakuni in Yamaguchi, and Sasebo in
Kyushu. It seems to me that there is a link between the free
spirit that surrounds the military bases, and the fact that
Tokyo Midtown and Roppongi Hills, another large mixed-use
development, attract lots of foreign tourists. In the Edo period,
these sites were home to *daimyō* mansions. Most of these
residences were built on high ground, where the view was
good and there was little chance of flooding, so the land is well
suited to this kind of redevelopment project.

The Suntory Museum of Art is one of the most popular
museums with overseas visitors to Japan. Its collections are
focused on the beauty that is found in everyday life, with its
holdings of ancient Japanese art and traditional handicrafts
among the best in the country. To give the building a sense of
the delicacy associated with such crafts, as well as a feeling
of warmth, I designed louvres from white porcelain panels, and
used them to cover the outer walls. The louvres are tapered, to
make their tips as fine as possible. (In fact, making tips as thin
as possible is one of my key design principles: the thin lip of a

SUNTORY MUSEUM

Vertical louvres on the façade control the light (above).
Inside, movable screens are controlled by a mechanism
inspired by traditional window design (overleaf).

48

teacup allows a better experience of the subtleties of tea –
this is always at the forefront of my mind when I pay such close
attention to edges.)

For the interior, I used paulownia wood, a wonderful
soft material that absorbs moisture, which is why it was used
for storing kimonos. Paulownia wardrobes were commonly
taken by a bride to her new husband's family home when she
got married. Another important choice of material was the
oak used for the floor. The Suntory distillery is known around
the world for its superior whisky, so I decided to make use of the
oak planks from their old barrels, applying heat to flatten them,
before laying them as floorboards. Some visitors say they can
still smell the whisky as they tread on them.

Inside the museum, we used *washi* (Japanese paper)
made by Yasuo Kobayashi, an artisan from Takayanagi (now
part of Kashiwazaki) in Niigata Prefecture. Kobayashi has his
own field, where he grows the *kozo* trees (a kind of mulberry)
used in making *washi*. In recent years, it has become common
to use *kozo* from Thailand or Taiwan, but Kobayashi believes
that this has resulted in a loss of the lustre *washi* originally
would have had when made from native *kozo*, so he decided to
grow his own. He also believes in the importance of the *suketa*,
a bamboo tray-shaped instrument used for straining the pulp
and spreading it thinly. By leaving a slight gap between the
bamboo sticks in the *suketa*, a finely striped pattern is created.
Kobayashi revived the practice of creating these delicate
stripes, which were always found in *washi* prior to the 1950s.

KITTE

As an in-house architect for the (now-defunct) Ministry of
Communications, Tetsurō Yoshida (1894–1956) designed
numerous splendid municipal buildings. One of his finest works,
the Tokyo Central Post Office (1931), has been revived by us as
the Kitte complex, combining office and commercial space
(we also transformed his Kyoto Central Telephone Office from
1926 into an Ace Hotel). While influenced by German modernist
architecture, Yoshida also produced designs that had more in
keeping with traditional Japanese wooden buildings. His work
was hugely influential, and it is in no small part thanks to him
that the design of Japan's post offices and telephone bureaus
remained of a consistently high standard.

    Yoshida was a close friend of Bruno Taut, who lived
in Japan in the 1930s, and assisted the German architect in the
design and construction of the only building Taut completed
in Japan, Hyuga Villa (1936) in Atami, Shizuoka Prefecture.
I designed the adjacent guest house Water/Glass (1995) as an
homage to Taut's Glass Pavilion, built for the 1914 Werkbund
Exhibition in Cologne, which established his reputation around
the world (it has since become the Atami Kaihourou hotel).

    When designing the Tokyo Central Post Office,
Yoshida incorporated beautiful octagonal columns as a way
of making the irregularly shaped plot workable. He understood
that by making the columns octagonal, minimizing the width
of each side, they would appear thinner than they actually
were. As a tribute to these columns, we fitted metal plates into
the central atrium in the place where they once stood and
recreated them using strings of metal beads. For the handrails,
we designed a pattern of fine silver stripes using a ceramic
print, as part of an interior space based around the motif of
the line. This harmonizes with Yoshida's original design and
his fondness for vertical lattices. Indeed, it was Yoshida who
brought the vertical lattice from traditional Japanese buildings
into the world of modernist architecture.

J P TOWER

53

In the commercial part of the facility, we decided to play on the building's former life as a post office. For the walls, we used interesting materials collected from all over Japan – wood, daub and metalwork – making them into rectangular boards reminiscent of postcards or envelopes, reinforcing the link to the old post office (the name of the building, *kitte*, also means 'stamp'). On the ground floor, we preserved the customer-service windows, and on the first floor is the annex of the Tokyo University Museum (the main building is in the Hongō campus). Here, fossils, specimens and other treasures owned by the university are on display.

On the third floor, the director's office has been preserved in its original state, and the view of the huge plated roof of Tokyo Station (1914), designed by Kingo Tatsuno (1854–1919), makes for an extremely impressive sight. It's said that Tatsuno's design was influenced by Centraal Station in Amsterdam. Tatsuno was also a huge fan of sumo wrestling, and the shape of the building, with its large wings to either side, may have been inspired by the pose assumed by *yokozuna* wrestlers as they enter the ring. The large roof, slightly baroque in feel, was destroyed by American air raids during the Second World War, but in 2014, under the guidance of Hiroyuki Suzuki, an architectural historian (and a former teacher of mine), the roof was restored to its original dynamic form.

Our design reinterprets Yoshida's octagon, creating a
'pillar of light' (above). Inside, we added glass handrails,
printed with a delicate pattern of thin lines.

55

SHINJUKU

Along with Shibuya (p. 12) and Ikebukuro (p. 64), Shinjuku is one of the major stations on the Yamanote line. It serves as a gateway to Tokyo's western suburbs, and the area around the station has the slightly anarchic feeling associated with the youth culture of that region.

Outside the eastern exit are two bar districts – Shinjuku Nichōme, the heart of Tokyo's gay culture, and a magnet for people from the worlds of the theatre and the arts, and Golden Gai – where one can truly experience the atmosphere of the Shōwa period (1926–1989). Also to the east is Shin-Ōkubo, a neighbourhood inhabited by non-Japanese Asian communities. Visitors looking for ethnic food or reasonably priced bars should head here, where the energy, diversity and vivacity of Japan's immigrant population can truly be experienced.

The western exit opens onto vistas that could have been designed by Le Corbusier, with high-rise office buildings towering above leafy parks. Originally, there was no town at all here, just a river: the Yodogawa. But from the

Visitors looking for ethnic food or reasonably priced bars should head to Shin-Ōkubo, where the energy, diversity and vivacity of Japan's immigrant communities can truly be experienced.

Today, skyscrapers are frowned upon in Japan, and are seen as the product of the mistaken mindset that prevailed during the country's period of enhanced growth.

1970s onwards, the area became home to the high-rise complexes that seem out of place in Japanese cities. By the 1980s, Shinjuku's western exit had become a showcase for Tokyo's architectural design scene.

The Tokyo Metropolitan Government Building (1990), designed by Kenzō Tange, is the area's tallest structure. The design of its twin towers – created at a time when Japan's economy was moving full steam ahead – was much discussed, with the building being compared to Notre Dame in Paris. Today, skyscrapers are frowned upon in Japan, and seen as the product of the mistaken mindset that prevailed during this period of enhanced growth. The two-tower design has also been much criticized as inefficient and prone to leaks.

Head further west and you come to an old fashioned-looking street, Jūniso-dōri ('street of the twelve shrines'). Here, you will find a more human, friendlier feel than in those parts of town littered with skyscrapers. Old hotels have been renovated, and cheap, delicious restaurants give new life to this old-style street.

MEJIRO

Mejiro is a station on the Yamanote line, and a district of Toshima, one of Tokyo's special wards. At the top of its plateau towers St Mary's Cathedral, designed by Kenzō Tange. It was completed in 1964, the year of the first Tokyo Olympics and the apotheosis of Tange's career as an architect.

Rather than designing a straight path into the cathedral from the street, as would normally be seen in religious buildings in the West, Tange instead created a dramatic entry that sends visitors to the back of the building, before turning around and ascending a staircase. This circuitous route into the cathedral, similar to the processional path to Meiji Jingū (see p. 24), reflects a particularly Japanese approach to design.

Tange's design, with its hyperbolic paraboloid thin-shell construction, was not only ground-breaking, but also structurally daring. Yoshikatsu Tsuboi, a fellow professor at Tokyo University, was the structural engineer for both the cathedral and the Yoyogi National Gymnasium (p. 8), which also had a distinctive suspended form. At the time, it was Tange's practice to create shapes that had not been seen before. The light pouring down from the ceiling in the cathedral is as dramatic as in the gymnasium, and worshippers and visitors alike find it very affecting.

Also on the plateau is the Eisei Bunko Museum, which exhibits art and artefacts once owned by the Hosokawa of Kokura (later Kumamoto), a family of *daimyō* with a rich history from the Kamakura period (1185–1333) to the present day. The eighteenth descendant, Morihiro Hosokawa, served as governor of Kumamoto and prime minister of Japan, before becoming a ceramicist. Nearby are the Wakeijuku student dorms, the setting for Haruki Murakami's novel, *Norwegian Wood* (1987). Murakami himself lived in the dorms while a student, and would travel down the hill to attend lectures at Waseda University.

Within the university campus is the Tsubouchi Memorial Theatre Museum, designed by Kenji Imai (1895–1987) in 1928 to resemble the seventeenth-century Fortune Playhouse in London. It is named for Tsubouchi Shōyō, who, like Imai, was a professor at Waseda. Next to the museum is our Waseda International House of Literature, which houses Murakami's books and record collection. In his novels, different times interconnect like a maze of tunnels, so we decided to convert this narrative structure into architecture, using wood as the primary material. Inside is a café where visitors can sip coffee while listening to the jazz that Murakami loved.

Next to the university is the distinctively shaped Kannon-ji Temple, designed by Osamu Ishiyama (b. 1944) in 1996, who taught for many years at Waseda. The university is known for its liberal style of education, of a quality to rival that of Tokyo University, and has produced many architects with a different style and philosophy to Tange, Isozaki, Maki and others from the Tōdai school. Tōgo Murano (1891–1984), who countered Tange's macho style with a feminine gracefulness, is a prime example of this, and Ishiyama himself, who championed self-build structures and the use of recycled materials, has also been hugely influential on the next generation.

Tange's design for the cathedral was not only ground-breaking, but also structurally daring ... The light pouring down from the ceiling is as dramatic as that seen in the Yoyogi National Gymnasium.

IKEBUKURO

Ikebukuro, in the north of the capital, has always been thought of as the roughest and most dangerous of Tokyo's principal stations, and, unlike Shibuya (p. 12) and Shinjuku (p. 56) seen as a shady part of town. This is particularly true of the area around its eastern exit, where Sugamo Prison – which counted political prisoners, dissenters and spies among its inmates – once stood.

At the beginning of the twenty-first century, as Japan's birthrate decreased, society became older, and the population in general grew smaller, towns and cities began to be labelled as 'at risk of extinction'. Ikebukuro was the only area in Tokyo that was deemed at risk, and became the focus of much negative discussion.

The local government of Toshima ward decided to flip the area's unsavoury reputation on its head, turning Ikebukuro into a destination known for its counterculture, which in turn would draw in young people. The person who initiated this great turnaround was the ward's mayor, Yukio Takano, a former secondhand bookshop owner.

We were asked to design a new ward office (ill. p. 67), to be located outside the station's eastern exit. This new type of multi-purpose space, combining housing with a town hall, and using solar panels and recycled wood panels, became a symbol of the neighbourhood. The random arrangement of small panels on the façade allows the building to blend into its surroundings. In the grounds was a cluster of small wooden houses, and nearby was a graveyard – this certainly wasn't an area with a good image, but our building changed all that.

The most memorable part of the design, the vertical 3D garden, is built up from ten layers. A small stream recycles rainwater and is home to tiny killifish, recreating the lush, peaceful nature that was typical in Tokyo in the past. Schoolchildren visit here and learn about the old ways, when people lived at one with nature.

Since the new ward office was completed in 2015, Minami Ikebukuro Park has also been restored, and is now the neighbourhood's answer to Central Park. With the previous regional office demolished, six theatres have been planned for the area, including one that will host *kabuki* performances and plays by the Takarazuka Revue, an all-female musical theatre troupe. Ikebukuro, which was once so distant from high culture of any kind, is in the process of being transformed into Tokyo's Broadway.

In contrast to the eastern exit, the western exit is more subdued. Jiyū Gakuen School (1921), designed by Frank Lloyd Wright, can be found here. Japanese architecture had a profound influence on Wright – who admired Japanese woodblock art and visited the country several times – particularly the traditional low-hanging eaves that project beyond the façades of buildings. In Wright's design for the school, the shadows created by these eaves are a major theme.

Wright used Ōya stone, a kind of soft and porous volcanic rock found near Utsunomiya, for both the Imperial Hotel (1923), opposite the Imperial Palace, and Jiyū Gakuen. We also used Ōya stone in our design for Hoshakuji Station (2008) in Takanezawa, near to the stone's extraction site. This was our homage to Wright, who valued the natural material of this location so highly.

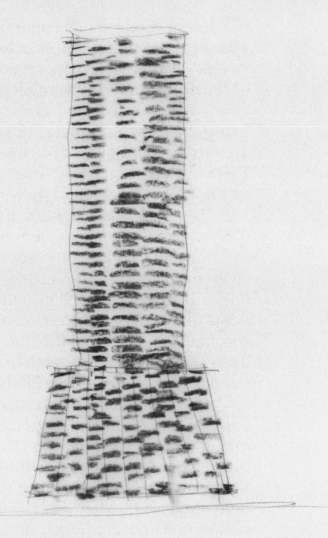

Toshima

UENO & YANESEN

In Edo-era Japan, much importance
was attached to the tenets of feng shui.
Temples were erected in certain areas
of towns and cities to ward off negative
energy, with the northwestern section
being the most auspicious, and the
area to the northeast being the worst.
This northeastern district was known
as the *kimon*, or 'demon's gate'.

In Tokyo, the neighbourhood
of Ueno lay in the *kimon*. To prevent
evil from flooding into the city, the
shogunate built a large temple,
Kan'ei-ji, in 1625, fronted by Shinobazu
Pond. In the Meiji era, Ueno Zoo (1882)
was built beside it, and the area grew
lively with visitors who came to see the
pandas brought over from China.

Ueno is also home to several
cultural venues and attractions,
including the Tokyo National Museum,
built in 1872 and inspired by the South
Kensington Museum (now the Victoria
and Albert) in London, and the Gallery
of Hōryū-ji Treasures (1999), designed
by Yoshio Taniguchi (b. 1937), which
contains objects from the collection
of the seventh-century Hōryū-ji

Temple in Nara. The International Library of Children's Literature (2000) and the National Archives of Modern Architecture (2013), both designed by Tadao Andō, can also be found here.

Ueno Station, which opened in 1883, was known as the 'gateway to Tokyo'. Agricultural labourers would arrive here from the Tōhoku region of Honshu Island, where the winters were too cold for farming. Having come south looking for work, a form of seasonal migrant labour known as *dekasegi*, they settled in Ueno. The Ameya-yokochō open-air market sprang up near the station, and is still bustling today. In the *Tora-san* series of films directed by Yōji Yamada, which depict life in Japan in the period immediately after the Second World War, the market (often abbreviated to 'Ame-yoko') appears many times.

A number of neighbourhoods in the city retain a working-class feel, reminiscent of Tokyo as it was in the old days. Yanaka, Nezu and Sendagi (known collectively as YaNeSen), in particular, is a good place to come to experience this, with many of the old houses converted into restaurants, hotels and galleries.

An artist friend, Bosco Sodi, who was drawn to the feel of the area, decided to convert one of the old wooden houses into a studio. The design was undertaken by Rafael Balboa, one of my students at Tokyo University. Nearby is one of the meccas of contemporary art, SCAI The Bathhouse, where Sodi hosts exhibitions from time to time. The gallery was converted from a public bathhouse, and its tiled curving roof, which used to indicate public baths, remains to this day.

In Edo-era Japan, much importance was attached to the tenets of feng shui, and temples were erected in certain areas of cities and towns to ward off negative energy.

JUGETSUDO KABUKI-ZA

During the Edo period, there were four theatres in Tokyo, for the performance of kabuki: Nakamuraza, Shimuraza, Moritaza and Yamamuraza. The ruling shogunate were wary of the art form, however, and imposed various restrictions, including limiting the width of the theatres to 5.5 m (nearly 18 ft). In 1889, the writer and critic Fukuchi Ōchi, along with the actor Ichikawa Danjūrō IX, decided that the new, modern Japan must create a theatre tradition that would amaze Western visitors, and therefore needed a new performing space, exclusively for kabuki, to rival the Opéra in Paris. The first *kabuki-za* was built, and came to be loved not only as a symbol of Japanese tradition and theatre, but also as the cultural heart of the districts of Ginza and Tsukiji.

After it was destroyed by fire in 1921, the theatre was rebuilt, but burned down again during the Great Kantō Earthquake of 1923. It was rebuilt in 1925, but this third version, too, was destroyed – this time by American air raids during the Second World War. The US occupation, led by General MacArthur, had initially considered banning kabuki altogether, but it was allowed to continue, thanks to MacArthur's aide-de-camp, Faubion Bowers, who ensured that a fourth *kabuki-za* was built in 1950.

When it was decided that this building needed updating to make it earthquake-resistant, we were commissioned to design a fifth version of the building. The exterior essentially follows the form of its predecessor, but we extended the eaves to augment the shadows, and exaggerated the design of the *karahafu* (a kind of undulating gable roof, unique to Japan), at the centre of the façade. The *karahafu* originally appeared in the third incarnation of the building, and was replicated in many of the public bathhouses built after the earthquake. Today, upon seeing a *karahafu*, most Japanese will either think of public baths or the *kabuki-za*. Until the Second World War, there were no baths in private homes, and public bathhouses formed a key part of everyday life, serving as a place for interaction and communication. Even today, there are over 500 public bathhouses remaining in Tokyo, giving one a taste of what life was like during the Edo period.

We also created a twenty-nine-storey tower behind the Jugetsudo Kabuki-za. For the front side of the tower, facing the theatre, we did away with conventional windows and instead created a three-dimensional façade with many shadows, drawing inspiration from the *nejiri renji kōshi* (narrowly spaced lattices with twisted bars) often observed in temples and shrines. The interior is designed in a vivid shade of scarlet known as '*kabuki-za* red', and a muted, dull gold.

The foyer boasts a hand-embroidered carpet created for the fourth *kabuki-za* in 1950, with a pattern featuring the Chinese phoenix, a sacred bird and the symbol of the building. The design is taken from the Phoenix Hall at Byōdō-in Temple in Uji, Kyoto, which appears on the ten-yen coin. The carpet is made by Oriental Carpet, a small Yamagata-based company, set up in 1935 to provide a place for unemployed women to work during the winter months in this snowy region (Yasunari Kawabata's novel *Snow Country*, published in 1937, was set in Yamagata), and they continue to produce handmade carpets to this day. On the roof is a Japanese garden, which is open to the public. A small museum faces onto it, where visitors can learn about the history of kabuki, and a café in which to enjoy green tea and Japanese sweets.

KABUKIZA

TSUKIJI & SHINBASHI

To the east of Ginza, Tokyo's largest downtown area, lies Tsukiji. Until 2018 it was the site of Japan's largest market, with lots of little shops and cafés (known as *jōgai*, or 'outside the market') surrounding it, which sold fish and seafood, traded wholesale inside. Even after the market moved to Toyosu, these *jōgai* remained open, retaining the area's bustling spirit, and there are still plenty of delicious, reasonably priced sushi restaurants to be found here.

Nearby is the headquarters of Japan's biggest advertising agency, Dentsu. When Kenzō Tange designed the original building in 1967, he was refining his 'Plan for Tokyo, 1960', a large-scale urban masterplan that featured an enormous floating city out in Tokyo Bay, offering a solution to the city's land-shortage problem. Tange put Tsukiji as the centre of his plan, which now seems grandiose and delusional. His design for the Dentsu building had much in common with the Metabolist philosophy of the 1960s, which maintained that buildings needed to continually evolve in a flexible way.

The current Dentsu headquarters (2002) was designed by Jean Nouvel, and features a distinctive curtain wall of ceramic printed glass. Nouvel was unhappy with the finished building, and refuses to acknowledge it as his own work. Today, it is now used solely by one of Dentsu's subsidiary companies.

Shinbashi, which lies to the south, was once famed for its geisha. The Japanese culture of inviting geisha to entertain guests with dancing and singing dates from the Edo period in the nineteenth century, and Shinbashi was its epicentre. As well as being a historic neighbourhood, it also looked to the future, and Japan's first railway was built here in 1872.

There are many tatami-floored restaurants (known as *ryotei*) in Shinbashi, with one of the most famous being Shinkiraku (1962). Designed by architect Isoya Yoshida (1894–1974), it combined the minimalism of Modernism with traditional wooden architecture. In its heyday, Shinkiraku was frequented by politicians and other public figures, and today it is where judging takes place for Japan's most prestigious literary award, the Akutagawa Prize.

Nearby is the Nakagin Capsule Tower (1972), designed by Kishō Kurokawa and comprised of re-arrangeable pods. Kurokawa, a former student of Kenzō Tange, was one of the founders of the Metabolist movement, which quickly came to worldwide attention and rocketed Kurokawa to fame as a young star of the architectural world.

With this building, Kurokawa's Metabolist philosophy was fully realized. After it was completed, however, it became almost impossible to switch over the capsules – indeed, since its completion, not one of the capsules has been moved. As a result, the Metabolist movement has been forgotten. Yet its core principles, which sought to draw architectural lessons from living organisms, has much inspiration to offer society today.

As well as being a historic neighbourhood, Shinbashi also looked to the future, and it was here that Japan's first railway was built in 1872.

TAKANAWA GATEWAY STATION

隈
研
吾
東
京

TAKANAWA GATEWAY

Takanawa Gateway is a new station designed by us, located on the Yamanote line between Shinagawa and Tamachi. It will probably be the last new station to be added to the line, which runs in a loop around the Imperial Palace, threading its way through the sloping land between the high and low areas of the city. Many of the stations have one entrance on the uphill side and another lower down, and the neighbourhoods around them have a totally different feel, depending on which exit you use to leave the station.

      The hilly areas in Tokyo are mostly made up of quiet, well-to-do residential districts, while the lower sections often have more of a populist feel, with shopping arcades and small urban factories. As a result, the atmosphere outside the entrances are dramatically different in character. Take the wrong exit, and you might find yourself lost in a completely different kind of neighbourhood than you were expecting. In Tokyo, elite and working-class cultures exist alongside one another and mix together. I think the fundamental cause of this is the complexity of the city's topography.

      A huge rail depot formerly stood where the station now stands. When it fell out of use, a new neighbourhood that would serve as a centre for Tokyo, halfway between Haneda Airport and Tokyo Station, was put forward. The station name arose from the fact that it would function as a 'gateway' to this new neighbourhood. The Chūō Shinkansen, a maglev line that will take passengers from Tokyo to Nagoya in just forty minutes, will arrive 100 m (328 ft) underground at Shinagawa, the next station along. The two stations are connected by a mall that spans between them, so the development around Takanawa station will also act as a gateway for passengers from the western part of Japan travelling on this super-fast train line.

      When designing the station, we knew we needed to create one that would be suitable for Tokyo as an international city of the twenty-first century, visited by people from around the world. To give them a sense of Japanese culture, we decided to cover the entire station with a large roof with

Takanawa Gateway Station, under construction (above), and
the 110 m (361 ft)-long roof, inspired by origami (overleaf).

geometric creases, resembling origami (overleaf). In most Japanese stations, the platforms and the main concourse have their own separate roofs, but here we used a single roof over the whole structure, which does away with the boundary between the station and the surrounding neighbourhood, creating a more fluid relationship between them. In the future, I believe that stations will be more like this, with the town and station becoming a single, unified space, where ticket barriers may no longer be necessary.

The large roof is supported by a frame constructed from a combination of metal and wood. The wooden frame is covered with a white translucent film, based on *shōji* screens. These sliding screens, made from *washi* paper stuck onto a wooden frame, represent what I like best about traditional Japanese architecture. In the wooden house where I grew up, built before the war, there were lots of these *shōji* screens.

In his essay *In Praise of Shadows*, Juni'chirō Tanizaki wrote about the effect of light and shadow, noting that light plays the main role in Western architecture, but in Japanese architecture, the gentle light that passes through *shōji* screens serves a key purpose. It reaches right to the back of the room, so that the space feels bright, even without the aid of artificial light. The soft light filtering through the white film at Takanawa Gateway Station represents a form of light that was forgotten about by Japanese Modernism.

LA KAGU

The neighbourhood of Kagurazaka is home to Japan's publishing industry. One company, Shinchosha, famous for publishing many of Haruki Murakami's novels, including *IQ84* (2009), asked us to convert their former warehouse into a multi-purpose building that would combine shop, café and lecture space. Much of our efforts went into the great wooden staircase, which we added outside the building. The warehouse was originally cut off from the road and difficult to access, but we re-connected them by placing a large, organically shaped staircase between the road and the warehouse, allowing the building to become part of the neighbourhood.

The topography of Kagurazaka is somewhat complex; the roads are narrow, and there are steep slopes and flights of steps that cars cannot drive down (the *-zaka* in 'Kagurazaka' means 'slope' or 'hill'). It occurred to me to use these hills as a way of expressing the culture and architecture of the neighbourhood. Tokyo is a city of hills, with most of it lying on an alluvial plain between the Tama and Kanda rivers. It is via these hills that the upland, elite neighbourhoods are connected with the more working-class areas down below. The slopes are thus a key part of the co-existence of these two worlds, used by people to come and go between them. Kagurazaka is particularly notable in this respect.

All of the wooden shelves used for storing books were on the warehouse's first floor. We decided to keep these shelves as they were to form a library, and we also created a small lecture hall for holding talks by writers and makers. Although contemporary society is moving away from books and towards computers and information technology, people nevertheless have a strong feeling of connection to – and nostalgia for – trees and things that are made from wood. La Kagu is a space where visitors can really get a sense of the culture of books. When they step inside, some even say that they can smell wood.

Near to La Kagu is SHAREyaraicho (2012), an apartment block designed for shared living, designed by my wife, the architect Satoko Shinohara (b. 1958). Kagurazaka is an old district that still retains the feel of the *hanamachi,* an area where geisha live and work, and recently, this nostalgic atmosphere has been gaining popularity among young people. Here, young artists and designers who are fond of the Kagurazaka neighbourhood can live alongside one another.

More and more buildings, designed explicitly for co-living, have been popping up all over Tokyo. The Japanese have not embraced house- and flat-sharing in the way that people do in the West, but in the last few decades this has begun to change. Prior to 1970, there were many *mokuchin aparto,* two-storey wooden apartment blocks that offered residents both low rents and a kind of co-living arrangement. It was common for youngsters who arrived in Tokyo from the provinces to live in these *mokuchin aparto,* and residents formed close relationships with their fellow tenants. But as Japan grew more affluent, this culture began to disappear. After the earthquake and tsunami of 2011, however, the *mokuchin aparto* tradition has been revived, and the practice of co-living is becoming popular again. These apartments offering co-living are known as *shea hausu* ('share houses').

Since the 1970s, owning a house or an apartment in the city has been seen as a symbol of wealth, sparking the appearance of medium-height concrete condominiums, which spoil the beauty of Tokyo. Since the tsunami, however, people have increasingly come to feel that sharing both spaces and things is better and easier than owning them, and SHAREyaraicho symbolizes that trend. There is a rooftop garden for growing vegetables and herbs, and the façade of the building is covered by a soft, semi-transparent sheet of fabric, giving it an entirely different feel to the coldness of concrete or glass condominiums.

LA KAGU

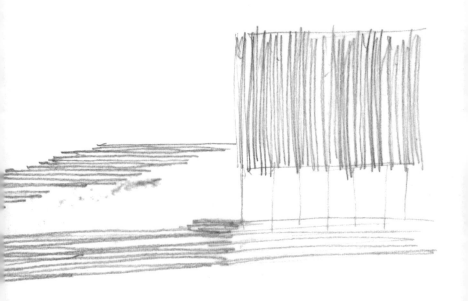

The external wooden staircase (overleaf).

AKAGI SHRINE

AKAGI SHRINE

Of all of the districts in Tokyo, it is Kagurazaka that is seen as still possessing the kind of narrow streets the city had in the past. The Akagi Shrine, believed to have been built around 1300, is situated in the middle of the neighbourhood. Its name derives from the view from the shrine to Mount Akagi, 150 km (93 miles) to the north, a sacred place where the gods were believed to live. Unfortunately, with all the buildings that have been built around the shrine, one can no longer see Mount Akagi from the grounds.

Historically, Japan's shrines have been built in order to worship the gods who live in the sacred mountains or seas; they don't reside in the shrine itself, but in the space beyond it. This belief that the spirits and deities exist beyond the confines of the shrine, and that the shrine itself acts not as a centre, but as a kind of gateway, is very different to the grand, imposing churches and cathedrals of Christianity.

The majority of shrines are not found in the mountains or in the middle of the fields, therefore, but at the borders of mountain villages – which is to say, at what is seen as the edge of the mountains. The *tori* gate, marking the entrance to a shrine, indicates that there are gods on the other side of it. When redesigning the Akagi Shrine complex in 2010, I also designed the *tori*, painting it in a comparatively pale shade of orange known as *mizu-urushi*. I felt that the traditional bright-red colour was overly forceful for the smaller, intimate feel of Kagurazaka.

During the first half of the twentieth century, Kagurazaka flourished as a *hanamachi*. For an *enkai*, a specific type of party held in traditional tatami-floored buildings, geisha would be invited through the *okiya* (geisha houses), and would dance and sing *nagauta* songs, accompanied by a *shamisen* (a three-stringed wooden instrument), and drink with the guests. This became seen as the most luxurious form of entertainment that could be had in Japan. There were several *hanamachi* in Tokyo, although the only ones left today are in Shinbashi, Akasaki and Kagurazaka. Even in Kagurazaka, the tradition has dwindled to the point of extinction. This seems to me a terrible shame. During the Edo period, *hanamachi* served as the epicentres of Kyoto and Tokyo culture, and it was thanks to them that the traditional dances and songs have survived.

With many of its low wooden buildings still remaining, Kagurazaka is beloved by artists and creatives. Director and screenwriter Yōji Yamada (see also p. 69) wrote his scripts in a room at Wakana, a *ryokan* (a traditional Japanese inn with tatami mats and communal baths) here. In 2020, we redesigned Wakana as a *ryōri-ryokan* (a *ryokan* specializing in food), but retaining its Japanese style. Hideki Ishikawa, one of Japan's most celebrated chefs, is in charge of catering, and guests can enjoy meals prepared by him in the comfort of their compact guest rooms, complete with bathtubs made from Japanese cypress. The room where Yamada wrote the *Tora-san* film series has been preserved as it was.

The entrance to the shrine, with the Park Court
Kagurazaka apartment building to the right (above).

DAIWA UBIQUITOUS COMPUTING
RESEARCH BUILDING

Of all the university campuses in Japan, the University of Tokyo
in Hongō is one of the oldest and most beautiful. The site
contains the ruins of the residence of the Maeda clan, a family
of *daimyō* from Kanazawa. The Akamon ('red gate'), a grand
lacquered gate built in 1827 to welcome the daughter of a
Tokugawa *shōgun* as a bride for one of the Maeda clan, is still
prized as a symbol of the campus.

When the Great Kantō Earthquake destroyed much
of the campus in 1923, and claimed the lives of over 100,000
people, Yoshikazu Uchida (1885–1972), an architecture professor,
was tasked with spearheading its reconstruction. He would
later go on to serve as chancellor of the university in the 1940s.
His son, Yoshichika Uchida (b. 1925), was my professor at the
University of Tokyo, and is one of the architects I have been
most influenced by. It was from him that I learned about the
brilliance of Japan's traditional wooden architecture.

At the same time that Frank Lloyd Wright was
designing the Imperial Hotel in the 1920s, Yoshikazu Uchida
was using scratch tiles made by artisans from Tokoname in
Aichi Prefecture across the entirety of the building façades
at the University of Tokyo, designing a distinctive canvas
that harmonized with the surrounding greenery. Thanks to
Wright's influence, the use of these tiles and Ōya stone became
widespread across Japan. Wright's choice of materials was
based on his belief that rough-textured materials that create
plenty of shadow were well suited to the country's scenery and
climate. His hunch proved to be correct.

When we set out to design a new research centre
for the IT department at the southern edge of the university
campus, we drew inspiration from the scratch tiles so beloved
of Wright and Uchida, creating a textured façade by using
hundreds of strips of cedar wood. Positioning the strips
randomly with gaps between them, we created four kinds of

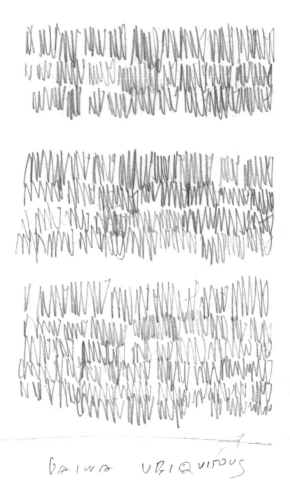

Detail of the façade, showing the strips of cedar wood
(above), and the interior of Haseko Kuma Hall (overleaf).

panels, which we overlapped like scales to give the building a gentle, organic feel, much like the hide of an animal. Precisely because it was to be a new centre for cutting-edge research, we felt that the use of soft, natural materials was appropriate. We created a large opening, which runs right through the centre of the building, to connect it with the garden of the Maeda residence and the rest of the campus. Next to the opening is a glass-fronted box, inside of which is a popular sweetshop run by Kurogi, one of Tokyo's best restaurants.

A statue of Josiah Conder, a British architect who arrived in Japan in 1877 to serve as professor for the Imperial College of Engineering (which later became part of the University of Tokyo), stands in the grounds. Influenced by the Arts and Crafts movement of the nineteenth century, Conder was fascinated by Japanese culture. At the time, Japan was looking to classical architecture of the West, rather than to its own traditional architecture, and he designed grand buildings in the European style for the elite of Japanese society, including the Mitsui Club (1913). Conder married a Japanese woman (and had an illegitimate child with a teacher of traditional dance), and studied *nihonga* (Japanese painting) under Kawanabe Kyōsai. Many of his paintings survive today.

Scattered across the University of Tokyo are buildings designed by architects who have taught here over the years: Kenzō Tange, Fumihiko Maki, Hisao Kōyama (b. 1937), Tadao Andō, and more. We were involved in renovating Haseko Kuma Hall and its foyer area on the ground floor of the Engineering Building, using wooden boxes, inside of which are displayed the university's latest research results.

WESTERN TOKYO

Western Tokyo is dotted with university campuses, some with buildings designed by notable architects. Tokyo Zokei University (1992) is positioned along an axis in a style that its architect, Arata Isozaki, clearly inherited from his teacher, Kenzō Tange, while Tama Art University Library (2007), designed by Toyo Ito (b. 1941), features rows of columns that recall Frank Lloyd Wright's Johnson Wax Headquarters (1936), in Racine, Wisconsin.

In his design for the Musashino Art University Library (2010), Sou Fujimoto (b. 1971) assigned the main role to the bookshelves. Fujimoto sees buildings as a conglomeration of small fittings and parts, and this library is an excellent example of that vision. At the International Christian University in Mitaka is the ICU Library (1960), designed by Antonin Raymond, who arrived in Tokyo to work as chief assistant to Wright during work on the Imperial Hotel, and remained in Japan after they parted company. Raymond went on to design many famous buildings, including St Luke's International Hospital (1928) in Tsukiji and St Alban's Church (1956) in Minato, and St Paul's Church (1935) in Karuizawa, Nagano Prefecture, becoming a hugely influential figure in Japanese architecture. Kunio Maekawa (1905–1986) and Junzō Yoshimura (1908–1997), leading architects of the Modernism movement in Japan, both worked in his studio.

Raymond preferred to design buildings in wood, and his work stands out from postwar Japanese architecture, which can seem like an endless sea of concrete. One of my first-ever clients, the industrialist Fusaichirō Inoue, was a patron of both Raymond and Bruno Taut. In the 1960s, he commissioned Raymond to design the Gunma Music Centre (1961) in Takasaki, and his own house was a copy of Raymond's home in Azabu, and was built with the architect's permission. This delicate wooden structure still stands, and is open to the public as the Takasaki Museum of Art. I was lucky enough to hear of his memories of Taut and Raymond in that very house.

Within the ICU campus is our New Physical Education Centre (2008), with its large wooden roof held up by folded plates that blend into the natural surroundings. This folded-plate structure was also used in Raymond's Gunma Music Centre, and was one of his favourite techniques.

In the Tokorozawa neighbourhood of western Tokyo, the publishing firm Kadokawa created a new cultural centre, which they asked us, together with Kajima Associates, to design. Combining a printing factory with a digital-printing system, a library, museum and a shrine, the centre – when completed – will be a new mecca for anime and other forms of Japanese subculture.

For the Kadokawa Culture Museum, which forms the heart of the building, we came up with a design that was modelled around an enormous rock. Next to the museum is the Ej Anime Hotel, which is themed around Japanese anime, and the Musashinonimasu Uruwashiki Yamatonomiyashiro shrine, which offers a new mix of subculture and high culture within a single facility in a way that would have been unthinkable in the past.

Fusaichirō Inoue, one of my first clients, was a patron of both Antonin Raymond and Bruno Taut ... His house is a copy of Raymond's home in Azabu, and is open to the public as the Takasaki Museum of Art.

ASAKUSA CULTURE TOURIST INFORMATION CENTRE

During the Edo period, Asakusa was one of the liveliest areas of Tokyo, and the heart of the metropolis until it was replaced by Ginza. The Sumida River, lined with *sakura* trees, ran along its east side. In the spring, when the cherry blossoms were out, the river banks grew crowded with people drinking and making merry as they admired the flowers. Today, people still come in cherry-blossom season to drink and sing until late at night.

In the centre of Asakusa is Sensō-ji, a temple built in 628 AD. It attracts thirty million visitors each year, making it the most-visited temple in Tokyo. Between the temple building and its main gate, the Kaminari-mon, lies a 300 m (984 ft)-long, two-storey shopping arcade – the Nakamise – which sells the kind of souvenirs and sweets that help give visitors a sense of what it was like in Edo-period Japan.

Across the road from the Kaminari-mon is our design for the Asakusa Culture Tourist Information Centre (2012). In the temple grounds is a five-storey pagoda (*gojūnotō*, or 'five-fold tower'), and to honour this, we designed the new centre in the form of a seven-storey pagoda. At 40 m (131 ft) tall, it has eaves at each storey, which join up with the interior. The façades are fixed with wooden louvres, which give a feeling of warmth and intimacy, whether you are on the ground floor or higher up. Unlike other tourist information centres, our design has a calm, serene atmosphere, so that visitors can feel truly at home. On the third floor is a small theatre, and on the top floor is a café with a terrace, where guests can sit with a beer and look down on the wind ruffling the Sumida River.

Unlike their Chinese counterparts, Japanese pagodas have deep, overhanging eaves. They were generally made from wood (whereas Chinese pagodas were made from brick or stone), and the extended eaves provided protection from the rain. Over time, pagoda design became perfected in Japan, and there are many beautiful examples, including the Hōryū-ji and

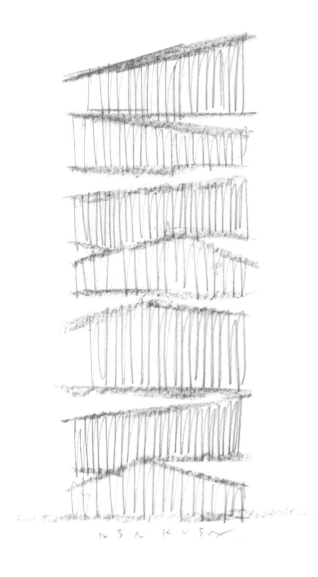

Hōshō-ji pagodas, and the Eastern Tower of the Yakushi-ji, all in Nara; the pagoda at Daigoji in Kyoto; and the Rurikō-ji pagoda in Yamaguchi. The Hōryū-ji pagoda, completed at the end of the seventh century, is the world's oldest wooden structure. When designing the new National Stadium (p. 42) for the Olympic Games, we were influenced by the pagoda technique of stacking eaves on top of one another to protect the wood.

On the opposite bank of the Sumida River lies the Asahi Beer headquarters (1989), a strange building with a golden sculpture mounted on top of a granite-plated black box. It was designed by Philippe Starck, and completed in 1989 when the Japanese economy was still going strong. The sculpture, with no clearly defined use, is a clear representation of its time. Today, the building is known as the 'golden poo', a reference to the shape of its crowning object.

The seven 'roofs' of the new Asakusa centre, with a
different activity beneath each one (above). Each floor
relates differently to the outside, giving each space
a unique character (overleaf).

MUKOJIMA

To the east of the Sumida River lies Mukojima, one of Tokyo's six *hanamachi*. These 'flower towns', or geisha districts, are in decline, as are the number of geisha, but business continues unabated in Mukojima. Comprising two elements, meaning 'across' and 'island', the neighbourhood's name refers to the fact that it lies on the other side of the river. The Sumida is a symbol of Tokyo, but is not like the Thames in London or the Seine in Paris, or other rivers that are woven into the geography of the city. Its banks were pushed back, so that the river became extremely wide and travelling across it feels liberating, like crossing the sea.

Inner-city *hanamachi*, such as Akasaka and Shinbashi, previously served as playgrounds for the establishment. From the 1990s onwards, however, the hospitality trade in Japan shifted, with people seeking increased levels of sophistication and politicians and public figures becoming far more cautious of the potential for media scandals, and the inner-city *hanamachi* began to dwindle in popularity.

But thanks to its location on the other side the river, Mukojima has been a place to be free from the cares of everyday life. It remained much loved and unaffected by the societal changes of the 1990s. Indeed, Mukojima has been described as a place that everyone could enjoy, 'from the Emperor to the tatami-maker' – a democratic experience that can be felt not just in the *hanamachi* district, but throughout the neighbourhood. It has proved popular with young people, who head to the shopping arcades here, where there are always new things going on.

Currently, there is a movement known as *rojison*, where people collect rainwater for use in the case of a natural disaster, which has attracted attention as a grassroots disaster-prevention strategy. *Roji–* means alley or narrow street, while *–son* is a suffix applied to the names of deities or the nobility, so *rojison* suggests a feeling of honouring the local streets. Mukojima is home to the Sumida Hokusai Museum (2016), designed by Kazuyo Sejima (b. 1956). Its sharp façade with aluminium panelling stands out from the muted, humble surroundings.

Travelling south along the river brings you to the Edo-Tokyo Museum (1993), designed by Kiyonori Kikutake (1928–2011) and Kishō Kurokawa. Kikutake is best known for his proposal to solve Tokyo's land shortage by reclaiming land from the sea, and using pilotis to elevate the buildings above the ground. For Expo 75 in Okinawa, he designed Aquapolis, a floating city supported by pilotis, which he also used in his design for the museum. These pilotis now seem an extension of that bubble-era mentality, with all of its attendant illusions of grandeur. With a declining population and increasing numbers of abandoned buildings, it seems somewhat misplaced and ridiculous.

Nearby is the Ryōgoku Sumo Hall (1985), where a two-week sumo championship is held three times each year, in January, May and September. It was designed by Takashi Imazato (b. 1928), a former student of Isoya Yoshida, the architect who created a new, distinctly Japanese style by blending traditional architecture with modernist principles.

Thanks to its location on the other side of the river, Mukojima has always been a place to be free from the cares of everyday life, and remains much loved and unaffected by the society changes of the 1990s.

TETCHAN

Harmonica Alley, which lies outside Kichijōji station on the Chūō line, is a curious place, established by squatters during the period of chaos and poverty after the Second World War. It takes its name from the way that the line of little shops, with their small entrances, give the street the look of a harmonica. In the period immediately after the war, it was something of a dangerous part of town, populated with brothels (at the time, Tokyo wasn't the regulated, safe city it is now).

Restaurateur Ichirō Tezuka is committed to ensuring that the atmosphere of Harmonica Alley is preserved, and asked us to design a branch of Tetchan, a *yakitori* restaurant, near its entrance. I was surprised by how small the budget was, but after visiting the warehouse of a renovation company, I decided to furnish the restaurant with the kinds of discarded items one wouldn't normally use in interior design, from recycled LAN cables to acrylic by-products. When designing another of Tezuka's restaurants, Amami, I used lots of logs with the bark still on them as an homage to the semi-tropical feel of Amami Island, which is close to Okinawa, but without its burgeoning tourist industry. Its natural surroundings and traditional culture remain untouched, making it a highly attractive place to visit.

Another part of Tokyo known for appealing alleyways is Shimokitazawa, which came second, after Arroios in Lisbon, in *Time Out*'s ranking of the coolest neighbourhoods in the world. Like New York's Brooklyn, Shimokitazawa is a young, fun-loving area, and cheaper than the more central parts of the city. We also designed two restaurants for Tezuka here: for one, we used discarded shop signs, and for the other, we created a façade from old aluminium sash windows and the interior from skis and snowboards. When using discarded objects in interior design, it gives even brand-new places the feeling that they have always been there. I think this is due to the inherent history of these thrown-away items, which lives on inside of them. This kind of recycled waste seemed the most appropriate building material for the area.

The reason Shimokitazawa evolved into such an interesting neighbourhood was that the two private railways passing through it – the Odakyū and Keiō lines – do not cross at right angles, but at an acute one, creating lots of 'static noise' in the form of level crossings and irregularly shaped plots of land. This area, full of static, wasn't suitable for large shopping centres or department stores, and instead became densely clustered with small boutiques, such as secondhand clothes shops, forming some of the most charming shopping streets in Tokyo.

The presence of small theatres such as Honda Gekijō and Ekimae Gekijō have also helped shape Shimokitazawa into the neighbourhood it has become. For a long time, the area was the haunt of youngsters from the world of the theatre. Before they make it on the stage, however, getting things cheaply is of primary importance – which is how Shimokitazawa came to be known for its reasonable prices. The Komaba campus of the University of Tokyo is nearby, and I would often go out drinking here as a student, lured by how cheap it was. In 2019, Shimokitazawa station was renovated. The tracks were replaced and a new station built, although, in a way, this preserved the area's 'static noise', so that its unique character has not vanished completely.

For the interior, we applied recycled LAN cables and melted acrylic by-products (above). The wall painting (overleaf) is by Teruhiko Yumura.

121

DIRECTORY

BUILDINGS BY KENGO KUMA & ASSOCIATES

Akagi Shrine [pp. 92–7]
Area: 4,069 m² (43,798 sq ft)
Completed: 2010

Asakusa Culture Tourist Information Centre
[pp. 108–13]
Area: 2,160 m² (23,250 sq ft)
Completed: 2012

Daiwa Ubiquitous Computing Research Building [pp. 98–103]
Area: 2,710 m² (29,170 sq ft)
Completed: 2014

ICU New Physical Education Centre [pp. 105–6]
Area: 5,966 m² (64,217 sq ft)
Completed: 2018

Jugetsudo Kabuki-za
[pp. 72–5]
Area: 127 m² (1,367 sq ft)
Completed: 2013

Kitte [pp. 52–5]
Design: Mitsubishi Jisho Sekkei
Area: 212,000 m²
(2,281,949 sq ft)
Completed: 2012

La Kagu [pp. 86–91]
Area: 962 m² (10,355 sq ft)
Completed: 2014

Meiji Jingū Museum [pp. 24–9]
Contractor: Shimizu Corporation
Structural engineer: Kanebako Structural Engineers
MEP engineer: P.T. Morimura & Associates, Ltd
Area: 3,200 m² (34,445 sq ft)
Completed: 2019

National Stadium
[pp. 6, 10, 42–5, 110]
Area 194,000 m²
(2,088,199 sq ft)
Completed: 2019

Nezu Museum [pp. 30–5]
Area: 4,014 m² (43,206 sq ft)
Completed: 2009

One@Tokyo [p. 18]
Area: 3,740 m² (40,257 sq ft)
Completed: 2017

One Omotesandō [pp. 20–3]
Area: 7,690 m² (82,774 sq ft)
Completed: 2003

Shibuya Scramble Square [pp. 13, 15]
Completed: 2019

Starbucks Reserve Roastery [pp. 18, 37]
Area: 3,187 m² (34,305 sq ft)
Completed: 2019

Sunny Hills [pp. 36–41]
Area: 297 m² (3,197 sq ft)
Completed: 2013

Suntory Museum of Art [pp. 46–51]
Area: 4,663 m² (50,192 sq ft)
Completed: 2007

Takanawa Gateway Station [pp. 80–5]
Construction began: 2015 (ongoing)

Tetchan [pp. 118–23]
Completed: 2014

Toshima Ward Office [pp. 65–7]
Design: Nihon Sekkei
Landscape: Landscape Plus
Lighting: Architectural Lighting Group
Signage: Terada Design
Area: 94,682 m² (1,019,147 sq ft)
Completed: 2015

Water/Glass [p. 52]
Area: 1,125 m² (12,109 sq ft)
Completed: 1995

BUILDINGS BY OTHER ARCHITECTS

Asahi Beer Hall [p. 110]
Architect: Philippe Starck
Completed: 1986

Christian Dior [p. 20]
Architect: SANAA
Completed: 2004

Dentsu Building [pp. 76–7]
Architect: Jean Nouvel
Completed: 2002

Edo-Tokyo Museum [p. 116]
Architects: Kiyonori Kikutake,
Kishō Kurokawa
Completed: 1993

Gallery of Hōryū-ji Treasures [p. 68]
Architect: Yoshio Taniguchi
Completed: 1999

Hillside Terrace [pp. 16–19, 38]
Architect: Fumihiko Maki
Completed: 1998

ICU Library [p. 104]
Architect: Antonin Raymond
Completed: 1960

Imperial Hotel [pp. 66, 98, 104]
Architect: Frank Lloyd Wright
Completed: 1923

International Library of Children's Literature [p. 69]
Architect: Tadao Andō
Completed: 2000

Jiyū Gakuen School [p. 66]
Architect: Frank Lloyd Wright
Completed: 1921

Kannon-ji Temple [p. 62]
Architect: Osamu Ishiyama
Completed: 1996

Komazawa Gymnasium [p. 8]
Architect: Yoshinobu Ashihara
Completed: 1964

Miu Miu [p. 20]
Architect: Herzog & de Meuron
Completed: 2015

Musashino Art University Library [p. 104]
Architect: Sou Fujimoto
Completed: 2010

Nakagin Capsule Tower [p. 78]
Architect: Kishō Kurokawa
Completed: 1972

National Archives of Modern Architecture [p. 69]
Architect: Tadao Andō
Completed: 2013

Neil Barrett [p. 20]
Architect: Zaha Hadid
Completed: 2008

Prada [p. 20]
Architect: Herzog & de Meuron
Completed: 2003

Ryōgoku Sumo Hall [p. 116]
Architect: Takashi Imazato
Completed: 1985

St Mary's Cathedral [pp. 60–1]
Architect: Kenzō Tange
Completed: 1964

SHAREyaraicho [p. 87]
Architect: Satoko Shinohara
Completed: 2012

Shinkiraku [p. 77]
Architect: Isoya Yoshida
Completed: 1962

Sumida Hokusai Museum [p. 115]
Architect: Kazuyo Sejima
Completed: 2016

Tama Art University Library [p. 104]
Architect: Toyo Ito
Completed: 2007

Tokyo Metropolitan Government Building [p. 59]
Architect: Kenzō Tange
Completed: 1990

Tokyo Skytree [p. 18]
Architect: Tadao Andō
Completed: 2011

Tokyo Zokei University [p. 104]
Architect: Arata Isozaki
Completed: 1992

Tsubouchi Memorial Theatre Museum [pp. 61–2]
Architect: Kenji Imai
Completed: 1928

Yoyogi National Gymnasium [pp. 8–11, 20, 42, 60, 63]
Architect: Kenzō Tange
Completed: 1964

ACKNOWLEDGMENTS

I wrote this book because I wanted to share my personal experience of Tokyo with visitors to the city. It would be wonderful if readers could explore Tokyo with this little book in hand, and make their own discoveries. I also touched upon relationships between the buildings I designed and their locations.

I would like to express my gratitude to Lucas Dietrich, Fleur Jones, Elain McAlpine, Poppy David and Ramon Pez at Thames & Hudson. My thanks also go to the staff of Kengo Kuma & Associates for putting together the text and materials necessary to help realize this project.

PHOTO CREDITS

Original drawings are by and courtesy of Kengo Kuma.

23 Mitsumasa Fujitsuka; **26, 28–9** Kobayashi Kenji Photograph Office; **33–5** Mitsumasa Fujitsuka; **39–41** Daichi Ano; **48, 50–1** Mitsumasa Fujitsuka; **55** Courtesy of Kengo Kuma & Associates; **82–5** Courtesy of Kengo Kuma & Associates; **90–1** Keishin Horikoshi; **95–7** Akagi Jinja; **100, 102–3** Takumi Ota; **111–13** Takeshi Yamagishi; **121–3** Erieta Attali

First published in the United Kingdom in 2021 by Thames & Hudson Ltd, 181A High Holborn, London WC1V 7QX

First published in the United States of America in 2021 by Thames & Hudson Inc., 500 Fifth Avenue, New York, New York 10110

Kengo Kuma: My Life as an Architect in Tokyo
© 2021 Thames & Hudson Ltd
Text © 2021 Kengo Kuma
Photographs and drawings © 2021 Kengo Kuma

Translated from the Japanese by Polly Barton

British Library Cataloguing-in-Publication Data
A catalogue record for this book is available from the British Library

Library of Congress Control Number 2019947789

ISBN 978-0-500-34361-6

Printed and bound in Italy by Printer Trento Srl

Be the first to know about our new releases, exclusive content and author events by visiting
thamesandhudson.com
thamesandhudsonusa.com
thamesandhudson.com.au

Kengo Kuma is one of Japan's leading architects and a professor in the Department of Architecture at the University of Tokyo. He is widely known as a prolific writer and philosopher and has designed many buildings in Japan and around the world, notably the Suntory Museum of Art in Tokyo, LVMH Group's Japan headquarters, Besançon Art Centre in France and the V&A Dundee in Scotland. Most recently, he designed the stadium for the Tokyo Olympics in 2021.